This book
belongs to:

_____

_____

Italy

© Copyright 2024 - All rights reserved.

The contents of this book may not be reproduced, duplicated, or transmitted without direct written permission from the author.

Under no circumstances will any legal responsibility or blame be held against the publisher for any reparation, damages, or monetary loss due to the information herein, either directly or indirectly.

Legal Notice:

You cannot amend, distribute, sell, use, quote, or paraphrase any part of the content within this book without the consent of the author.

Disclaimer Notice:

Please note the information contained within this document is for educational and entertainment purposes only. No warranties of any kind are expressed or implied. Readers acknowledge that the author is not engaging in the rendering of legal, financial, medical, or professional advice. Please consult a licensed professional before attempting any techniques outlined in this book.
By reading this document, the reader agrees that under no circumstances is the author responsible for any losses, direct or indirect, which are incurred as a result of the use of the information contained within this document, including, but not limited to errors, omissions, or inaccuracies.

TABLE OF CONTENTS

Introduction
- Your Roman Adventure Starts Here
- How to Use This Travel Guide

Journal Prompts – Before you Arrive

PART I — Adventures in Ancient Rome

The Rise & Fall of the Colosseum
- Exploring the largest amphitheatre in the world

Take a Walk Through the Real Ancient Rome
- Exploring the Roman Forum

Find Top Five Treasures at the Roman Forum
- Ancient artefact treasure hunt

The Pantheon Temple of All Gods
- Exploring Ancient Rome's best preserved building

Vatican City & St. Peter's Basilica
- Spot the Angels in St. Peter's Square

Michelangelo's Sistine Chapel Masterpiece
- Colour the Ceiling Like Michelangelo

Make a Wish at Trevi Fountain
- Toss a coin for luck and learn fun facts about the place where three roads meet

PART II — Museums, Ancient Artefacts & Modern Art in Rome

Art and Ancient Artefacts at the Vatican
- Art Detective Scavenger Hunt in the Vatican Museums

The Inspiring Italian Masterpieces of Galleria Borghese
- Match the Statues Challenge

Capitoline Hill & Rome's Oldest Museums
- Ancient Treasure Hunt

National Roman Museum
- Slices of Ancient Roman Life at Museo Nazionale Romano

The MAXXI Museum of Modern Art
- Spot the Shapes

PART III — Adventures with Animals and Oranges in Roman Gardens

Escape to Villa Borghese Gardens
- Wildlife spotting challenge

Spy on the Vatican in the Orange Garden
- Find the oldest orange tree and secret peep hole

A-Maze-ing Villa Doria Pamphili Gardens
- Picnic Spot Challenge

Exotic Encounters at Bioparco Zoo
- Play Animal Tracker

PART IV — Fortresses and Bravery Challenges

Hadrian's Mausoleum
- Fortress Exploring Adventure

Treasure Hunting in the Catacombs of Rome
- Earn Yourself a Catacomb Bravery Badge

Dare You Test the Mouth of Truth?
- Put your hand in the lie-detecting mouth

PART V — Pizza, Pasta & The World's First Ice Cream

Gelato Fit for a Duke
- Gelato Taste Test Adventure

A Slice of History Pizza
- Rate Your Favorite Toppings

Prehistoric Pasta Dinners in 300 BC
- Rate Rome's Most Perfect Pasta

Local Life at the Morning Market
- Foodie Treasure Hunt

Pastries and Cannoli: Sweet Surprises
- Dessert Critic Challenge: Rate Your Favorites

PART VI — Getting Around Rome Like a Pro

Boarding Buses and the Metro
- Rome Bus Routes and metro maps

Vespas: The Wasps of Rome
- Buzzing around Rome on two wheels

Taxi Hailing Tips
- Types of Taxis & Taxi Etiquette

Bridges and Boat Rides on the Tiber River
- Walk across the oldest Roman bridge

PART VII — Getting Acquainted with Real Roman Culture

Italian Theater: From Opera to Street Performances
- The evolution of the Italian art scene

The Artists and Fountains of Piazza Navona
- Baroque water sculptures

Across the Tiber to Timeless Trastevere
- Explore an ancient Roman neighborhood

Italian Slang for Kids
- Talk Like a real Roman

Rome's Modern Murals & Street Art
- Artistic graffiti

PART VIII — Day Trips and Excursions from Rome

Frozen in Time Under the Ashes of Pompeii
- Explore the town swallowed by a volcano

Emperor Hadrian's Villa and Palaces
- Royal Explorer Game in Hadrian's Villa

Exploring Enchanting Castles
- Old Roman camps and castrum

Ostia Antica - The Oldest Seaport
- Tranquility on the coast

PART IX — Fun Rome Facts and Trivia

- **Mind-Boggling Rome Trivia to Impress Your Friends**
- **Famous Roman Rulers and Artists**
- **Strange Roman Laws and Traditions**
- **The Legend of Wolf Children Romulus and Remus**

PART X: Creating Your Own Roman Adventure

- Make Your Own Rome Scrapbook
- Roman Memory Lane Journal Prompts
- Design Your Own Roman Crest or Shield
- Draw Your Favorite Roman Landmark
- Write a Postcard to Your Future Self
- Plan Your Next Roman Adventure
- More Memory Lane Journal Prompts

Appendix

A. Useful Italian Phrases for Young Travelers

B. Recommended Books and Movies About Rome for Kids

YOUR ROMAN ADVENTURE STARTS HERE

Rome, the capital of Italy, is the best destination for history buffs and budding archeologists. The city has the highest concentration of historical, archaeological, and architectural heritage in the world, transporting you to a glorious era of chariot-racing gladiators and megalithic temples dedicated to mythological gods.

Many of the ancient ruins you'll explore in Rome are so important that they are UNESCO World Heritage Sites, ensuring they are preserved for future generations to wander in awe at their splendor.

Famous landmarks such as the Colosseum and the Pantheon are among the most famous wonders of the world that you'll see in Rome. By the end of this guide and your Roman adventure, you'll know a lot more than most about these very special places.

HOW TO USE THIS TRAVEL GUIDE

This fun travel guide is packed with games, facts, tips and tricks to help you make the most of your trip to Rome as you explore iconic historical places in the capital of Italy and beyond.

The book is divided into ten parts, each giving you information, insight and inspiration for your adventure into the past, where gladiators fought to the death and Roman emperors ruled the world, as well as other historical places such as Pompeii, which was buried by a volcano that is still active today.

Rome ranks among the top ten cities in the world with the most museums, numbering almost 100 in total. You won't have time to see them all, of course, but you can use the pointers in these pages to find the most fascinating museums and the most historical artefacts in them.

With this book in hand, write about your expectations before your Rome visit, record fun facts you find out along the way, and tell us about your adventures after your return.

BEFORE YOU ARRIVE IN ROME JOURNAL PROMPTS

1. Write a few lines explaining what you are most excited about seeing or doing in Rome.

_____
_____
_____
_____
_____
_____
_____

2. List some of the items you've packed or plan to pack for your Rome trip.

_____
_____
_____
_____
_____
_____
_____

3. Tell us who you are going to Rome with. Are you visiting with family and friends or on a school trip?

_____
_____
_____
_____
_____
_____
_____

4. Look at a map of Rome and write about the places you want to visit and why.

_____
_____
_____
_____
_____
_____
_____
_____

5. What historical event or figure in Rome are you most interested in learning more about?

Rome

6. Tell us some things that you already know about ancient Rome.

7. What famous Rome landmarks are you excited to see?
   Draw a picture of one and write why it's interesting to you.

DRAW HERE

8. What foods are you excited to try while you're in Rome and what do you think they'll taste like?

_____
_____
_____
_____
_____
_____
_____

9. Rome is full of history and art. What different cultures or time periods are you hoping to learn about while you're there?

_____
_____
_____
_____
_____
_____
_____

10. What do you hope to learn or experience on your trip to Rome? Write about what you think the city will be like.

_____
_____
_____
_____
_____
_____

PART I

Adventures in Ancient Rome

Let's go 2,000 years back in time as we explore the megalithic ruins of Ancient Rome hunting for treasures in temples dedicated to mythological gods, plus Vatican City, where the walls and ceilings are adorned with the world's most revered artwork.

The Rise & Fall of the Colosseum

The Colosseum was, and still is, the largest amphitheater in the world. It's so big that you could fit three American football fields inside its walls!

The Colosseum's name comes from the Greek word for 'giant' (kolossos). And 'amphitheater' means 'round' or 'oval theatre'. When it was built about 2,000 years ago, the amphitheater could hold 50,000 spectators to watch plays, chariot races, gory gladiator battles and fights to the death between men and ferocious beasts.

The Colosseum was a gift to the people of Rome from Emperor Vespasian, considered Rome's greatest emperor. Entertainment also featured reenactments of naval battles. And even gorier than the gladiator battles were the executions called 'condemnation to beasts' in which criminals were devoured by animals.

Standing at around 513 feet tall and roughly 620 feet wide in the center of Rome, the Colosseum is a shadow of its former glory, after an earthquake in 1349 caused one of its sides and several arches to collapse.

Entry into the Colosseum is free for children under 18 and seniors over 65 from the EU. Other visitors must buy entry tickets.

Take a Walk Through the Real Ancient Rome

The imposing pillars and temple ruins of the ancient Roman Forum are the remains of the center of Ancient Rome. Details of its history are sketchy but the Roman Forum is said to have been a massive open-air market place and the seat of Rome's politics and religion, similar to today's Houses of Parliament and stately buildings of central London, or Washington DC's Capitol Hill and the Lincoln Memorial.

The ancient Romans worshipped several different gods, many of them named after planets, building gigantic monuments such as the Temple of Saturn and the Temple of Venus and Roma. Walking among the Roman Forum ruins, you can discover ancient stone arches and pillars, basilicas, prisons and palaces, plus pools, springs, cobbled streets and staircases.

The first buildings of the Roman Forum are said to have been built around 750 BC but today they lie in ruin following the fall of the Roman Empire about 1,500 years ago in 476 AD.

Exploring the Roman Forum. Entry is free for children under 18 but adults must buy a ticket.

Entry is free for all on the first Sunday of the month, but expect long queues.

Find Top Five Treasures at the Roman Forum

Exploring the Roman Forum is like an Indiana Jones adventure with mystery and mythology around every corner. Grab a free tourist map and find these awesome top-five treasures along the trail:

Curia Julia's Mosaic Floor
The old Senate House of ancient Rome, Curia Julia, has a spectacular mosaic floor of marble in geometric patterns.

Statues of the Vestal Virgins
Standing guard at the House of the Vestal Virgins, the row of statues were Rome's most powerful women and revered keepers of the city's sacred flame.

Head, hands and feet of the Statue of Constantine
Find the massive marble head, hands, and feet of the Statue of Constantine, which once stood over 15 meters high, in the museums on Capitoline Hill.

Carvings on the Arch of Titus
Look at the underside of the Arch of Titus to see military conquests by Roman legions carved into the stone in fascinating detail.

The Temple of Saturn
Only eight granite columns remain at the ancient site of the Temple of Saturn, which represented Rome's enormous wealth and was a repository for the State treasury.

The Pantheon Temple of All Gods

The Pantheon is one of Ancient Rome's oldest mega monuments and it's still miraculously intact. In fact, it's even older than the Colosseum, but its origins remain a mystery as no one really knows who built it and why.

'Pantheon' is a Greek word meaning 'temple of all gods'. Step through the Pantheon's giant bronze doors into a vast domed space created as a home for the gods Jupiter, Saturn, Pluto, and Venus.

The Pantheon's dome is one of the largest in the world, spanning over 43 meters and rising more than 20 meters. Sunlight shines through a hole in the dome called the 'Eye of the Pantheon', or 'Oculus'.

See if you can find the things that represent the gods in the Pantheon. Jupiter is represented by an eagle holding a thunderbolt in its claws.

Saturn was the god of harvest and plenty. Pluto was the god of the underworld, represented by a scepter or a key, and sometimes a three-headed dog. Venus is a female. She's the goddess of love, beauty, fertility, and victory, often depicted standing in a seashell.

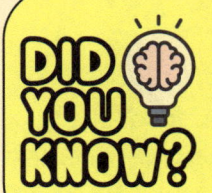

DID YOU KNOW? The Pantheon's bronze doors weigh about 20 tons each, making them the largest ancient bronze doors in existence.

Vatican City & St. Peter's Basilica

Vatican City is the center of the Roman Catholic Church and the smallest sovereign state in the world. The Pope lives here and is protected by a small army of Swiss guards in striking red, blue, and yellow uniforms.

There are six main marvelous attractions to explore in Vatican City, starting with Saint Peter's Square (Piazza San Pietro). An ancient Egyptian obelisk decorated with hieroglyphs stands 25 meters tall in the square. Across the piazza stands St. Peter's Basilica with a magnificent dome, the Treasure Museum, the Necropolis, and the Sistine Chapel.

The basilica is an ornately decorated cathedral adorned with marble mosaics, paintings and tapestries. The basilica's dome is a masterpiece of artistic Renaissance architecture from which is a stunning view across Rome.

Inside the Treasure Museum you can see a collection of priceless ancient treasures and centuries-old artwork. Underneath the Basilica you can explore the old streets of the 'city of the dead', the Necropolis.

Lastly, the Sistine Chapel is the most magnificent and awe-inspiring attraction to explore in Vatican City with its famous walls and ceiling, painted by Michelangelo di Lodovico Buonarroti Simoni more than 500 years ago (between 1508 and 1512).

You can take guided audio tours around the different attractions in Vatican City. Allow at least an hour for each part that you visit. Entry into St. Peter's square is free but you'll have to buy tickets to enter the museums.

Spot the Angels!

There are over a hundred statues in Vatican City's St. Peter's Square. Some of them are ancient carvings of Catholic saints, including large statues of St. Peter and St. Paul. Many of the statues are angels, easily recognizable by their wings. How many angels can you spot in the square?

There's also a new statue depicting 140 migrants fleeing Nazi Germany in a boat called Angels Unaware. The sculpture was unveiled in 2019 to mark the 105th World Day of Migrants and Refugees. The figures are amazingly lifelike. Can you spot Christ's parents, Mary and Joseph, among the refugees, and a pair of angel wings?

The Angels Unaware statue was inspired by the bible passage: "Do not forget to show hospitality to strangers, for by so doing some people have shown hospitality to angels without knowing it".

Michelangelo's Sistine Chapel Masterpiece

The world's most famous frescoes

From the outside, the Sistine Chapel looks somewhat ordinary but once inside, you can see for yourself why this corner of Vatican City is so famous and revered as a testament to Renaissance art and architecture.

You'll be awestruck by the depictions of biblical scenes painted on the walls and ceiling of the chapel by 16th-century artist and sculptor Michelangelo. Look up to see the most famous painting of all, the Creation of Adam, showing the hands of God and Adam, which is among nine scenes from the Book of Genesis painted by Michelangelo.

Many other artworks adorn the chapel walls, including tapestries depicting the gospels by Italian artist Raffaello Sanzio da Urbino.

As well as being a museum, the Sistine Chapel plays host to a variety of important religious occasions, including the nominations of new Popes.

You could days admiring all the details of the paintings and tapestries in the vast chapel, which is so large that it once took 10 years to clean all the dust and grime.

Colour the Ceiling Like Michelangelo

When Michelangelo painted the ceiling of the Sistine Chapel, he had to lie on his back on scaffolding raised to the ceiling. Isn't it amazing that he could paint so perfectly in such a precarious position?

You could try this yourself and see if you have what it takes to paint while lying down, just like Michelangelo, but not on the ceiling! Instead, you can paint lying under a low desk or table. Here's what you need:

- A desk or table
- Pieces of paper to paint on
- Masking tape to stick the paper to the underside of your desk or table
- Art supplies of your choice
- An old sheet to put on the floor and lie on

Think about whether you will use paint, crayons, pencils or pens to create your table ceiling masterpiece. If you use paints, be prepared to get your face splattered with drops pf paint. That's why you need an old sheet to lie on so you don't get paint on the floor or carpet!

Make a Wish at Trevi Fountain

Where Roman roads meet and fresh water flows

Trevi Fountain is a wonderfully artistic blend of flowing water and splendid sculptures depicting mythological scenes around a pool, where visitors toss in coins for good luck. It's the largest fountain in Rome, standing over 26 meters tall, and widely considered the most exquisite Baroque structures in the world.

Historians believe 'Trevi' is from the Latin word 'trivium', meaning 'the place where three roads meet'. The fountain stands at end of an ancient Roman aqueduct called Aqua Virgo, which fed fresh spring water from the countryside.

The many statues surrounding the fountain celebrate the life-giving properties of water with Oceanus, God and Titan of Water, surrounded by the statues of Abundance, Salubrity, Tritons and Hippocamps. Can you spot a cherub and the winged water horse Pegasus?

Toss in a Coin for Luck

According to folklore, tossing a coin into the Trevi Fountain pool will make your wishes come true, and even bring you back to Rome one day, but you must toss your coin in the traditional way to ensure it brings you good luck! Here's how to do it correctly:

Place a coin in the palm of your right hand and turn your back to the fountain. Then toss the coin over your left shoulder as you make your wish. You'll also bring luck to someone else less fortunate as the coins tossed into the fountain are donated to charity.

PART II

Museums, Ancient Artefacts & Modern Art in Rome

Let's see what treasures are stashed away inside Rome's most famous museums and galleries filled with art through the ages, from the Italian Renaissance up to modern times.

Art and Ancient Artefacts at the Vatican

Being the capital of Italy, Rome is home to some of the world's most stunning art, literature and architecture created during the Renaissance in the early 1500s, as well as many historical artefacts from foreign lands brought to Rome during the thousand-year reign of the Roman Empire from 753 BC to 476 CE.

Some of the most revered works of art in Rome, including paintings and sculptures, are kept in the Vatican's 54 museums, which between them house about 70,000 works of art! Only about 20,000 of those artworks are on public display, but that's still a staggering amount and you probably won't be able to see them all in one visit!

As well as decorating the Sistine Chapel, Italian Renaissance artist Raphael and his students painted four rooms in the Vatican Museums known as the Raphael Rooms, each decorated with frescoes illustrating myths and legends such as the *Battle of the Milvian Bridge*, the *Mass at Bolsena*, and the *Victory of Christianity Over Paganism*.

Painted between 1508 and 1524, the four Raphael Rooms are called Room of Constantine, Room of Heliodorus, Room of the Segnatura, and Room of the Fire in the Borgo.

In the Vatican Gallery of Maps, find the cartography collection of Italian mathematician, astronomer, and cosmographer Ignazio Danti. If mummies and hieroglyphs are your thing, then visit the Gregorian Egyptian Museum.

Vatican museums are open Monday to Saturday from 8.30am to 6.30pm (last entry 4.30pm).

Art Scavenger Hunt

With more than 50 museums spanning more than nine miles in Vatican City, there's no way you can see them all, so here's a list of some of the museums and the artefacts you can find in them so you can take your pick for an art scavenger hunt.

Apollo Belvedere – a marble sculpture regarded as one of the supreme masterpieces of world art and the absolute standard for male beauty, found in the Pio Clementino Museum.

Augustus of Prima Porta – a two-meter tall marble sculpture of Augustus, the first Roman emperor, unearthed from an ancient Roman villa just outside Rome, found in the New Wing.

Julius Caesar – a marble statue of probably the most famous Roman general and statesman, who transformed the Roman Republic into the Roman Empire, found in the Gregoriano Profano Museum.

L'Annuncio – a painting by world-renowned modern artist Salvador Dalí, who said "My best ideas come through my dreams", found at the Collection of Modern and Contemporary Art.

Phoenix Crown – an ornament from ancient China, worn by women of the imperial court, found in the Ethnological Museum.

Sphere Within Sphere – a large bronze globe with a futuristic look and a mechanism inside that rotates with the wind, found outdoors in the Pinecone Courtyard.

Galleria Borghese: Art of the Italian Masters

Rome, as well as Italy as a whole, is the site of many famous works of art, as well as the home of the people who created them, including Da Vinci, Michelangelo, and Raphael. And no one appreciates this art more than the Romans themselves!

Indeed, around 1605, an Italian cardinal by the name of Scipione Borghese commissioned the construction of Galleria Borghese, which was designed specifically to house the many pieces of art he had collected over the years. These ranged from pieces he had purchased from the leading artists of his time as well as others from various parts of Europe.

It took some time for the Galleria Borghese to be opened to the public! In fact, it was only around 1902 when the gallery and the surrounding park were sold to the Italian government that people were allowed to visit.

Today, the gallery welcomes more than 500,000 people every year!

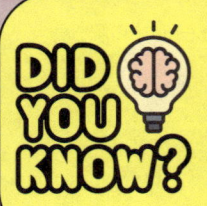

> **DID YOU KNOW?** At its peak in AD 117, the Roman Empire ruled over about 100 million people (20% of the world's population) in 50 different countries covering 4.4 million square kilometers.

Match the Statue!

Roman renaissance sculptures of human figures are amazingly accurate and detailed studies of human anatomy. The poses and expressions are like snapshots of historical and mythological events with a story behind every line, right down to the mussels, veins and frown lines on foreheads.

When you see a bust or statue, see if you can tell by the pose and facial expression what emotions the sculptor wanted to portray.

Then have a go at recreating the statue by mimicking the pose and expression. It's art after all, and it's all about individual expression.

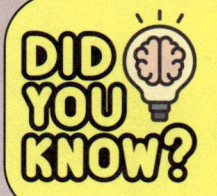

DID YOU KNOW? Ancient stone is everywhere in Rome. The city is home to a total of 82 temples and about 50,000 statues.

Capitoline Hill & Rome's Oldest Museums

Atop one of the 'Seven Hills of Rome', among the pillars and ruins of the ancient Roman Forum, sit Rome's oldest museums, the Capitoline Museums, housing the oldest collections of art available for public viewing in the world.

The largest and most important temple in Ancient Rome, the Temple of Jupiter Optimus Maximus, once stood on this hilltop, marking the capital of Rome just as Capitol Hill and the surrounding monuments in Washington DC denote the capital of the USA.

Today the Capitoline Museums are a treasure trove of ancient sculptures, paintings, coins, jewelry and archaeological finds dating back thousands of years. Here you'll see how ancient Rome looked in its former glory with scale models of the temples, giving you a bird's-eye view of the old capital, as well as the world's oldest bronze sculptures, which are more than 2,000 years old!

You might recognize some of the characters from Greek and Roman mythology such as Hercules the god of strength, and Medusa the goddess with a living snakes in place of hair, whose stare turned anyone who looked at her to stone.

The Capitoline Museums actually comprises two buildings, which are connected by an underground tunnel beneath Campidoglio Square, which was designed by Michelangelo.

One of the most famous bronze statues, because of its age and imagery, is Romulus and Remus; Rome's founders, feeding from their she-wolf mother (more on page 67).

Ancient Treasure Hunt

The Capitoline Museums contain artwork spanning millennia, with statues, carvings and paintings that are a few hundred years old to some over 2,000 years old, predating historical records. Many treasures are shrouded in mystery and considered priceless relics that can never be sold, no matter how high the bids go.

Take a pen and notebook with you as you wander through the museums so you can make a list of artefacts from the newest to the oldest by writing down its name and the year it was made.

See if you can be the first among your friends or family to find the very oldest artefact.

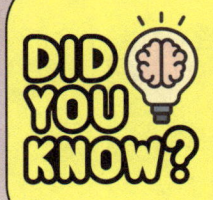

DID YOU KNOW? The ancient Romans lived during the Bronze Age. They were experts at crafting ornaments and lifelike statues from materials such as gold, silver, iron, bronze, and stone.

25

National Roman Museum

Slices of Ancient Roman Life at Museo Nazionale Romano

You can find even more ancient archeology discovered after the fall of the Roman Empire in the buildings of a 15th-century palace that is now home to the National Roman Museum.

Here you can see a real mummy inside a richly decorated sarcophagus with several artefacts in amber and pieces of jewelry, as well as Renaissance artworks and antiquities, Greek and Roman sculptures, plus a library of ancient books that could contain secret recipes for elixirs and magic spells, if only we could decipher them!

Wandering around the four giant buildings of the National Roman Museum you get a really good feel for what life was like in Ancient Rome thousands of years ago.

History Detective Challenge

It's time to don your dusty Indiana Jones hat and grab your trusty whip and a notebook for a History Detective Challenge in the National Roman Museum. Get ready to write down the details of artefacts catching your eye.

The most important questions any good detective asks are What, Where, When, Who and Why?

See if you can find out the story behind a statue so you can report your findings after your visit. The one with the best story wins!

Who knows, it could be the plot for a blockbuster book or movie about archaeological adventures!

The MAXXI Museum of Modern Art

Now for something completely different! If you've seen enough of the old stuff in Rome's museums, head over to the MAXXI Museum – a space-age looking building that could pass as a base on the moon, where you'll find only modern twenty-first century art in all shapes and sizes.

MAXXI Museum certainly stands out among the older buildings as a showcase of modern Italian architecture and technology to form overlapping platforms of glass, concrete, and steel. The interactive exhibitions inside let you become part of the architecture and experience the effects of light and form as you walk around.

Exhibitions change with the times to show off the latest inspirations of the newest artists and architects on the scene.

The museum is closed on Mondays and open Tuesday to Sunday from 11:00am to 7:00pm. Entry is free for children aged under 18 years old.

Spot the Shapes!

The trendy architecture of MAXXI museum is a smart blend of different geometric shapes, some smooth and some with sharp edges, but they all seem to blend together in an eye-catching, artistic way for a futuristic look and feel.

See if you can make a list or drawings of all the different geometrical shapes you can see and count the number of them you find.

PART III

Adventures with Animals and Oranges in Roman Gardens

Let's enjoy the sunny side of Rome's outdoor attractions, gorgeous gardens and pretty parks.

Escape to Villa Borghese Gardens

The gardens around Villa Borghese (see page 22) are a beautiful landscape that transports you back in time to a lush version of ancient Rome with temples nestled among the trees and reflected on the sparkling ponds.

The gardens cover more than three miles. You can explore on foot or by renting a bike to see the garden's many fountains and statues. The Temple of Aesculapius is one of the most stunning features found in the Villa Borghese gardens. It's said to be a recreation of the ancient temple to the god of Medicine.

There's also a zoo nearby (see page 32), and you can rent boats to paddle across the lake. Entry to this public park is free for all. The park is open to all every day from dawn until dusk.

Wildlife Spotting Challenge

Many species of birds, mammals, insects and even lizards live among the bushes and trees around the lakes of Borghese Gardens.

See if you can spot some of the rarer inhabitants such as the Great Spotted Woodpecker, Kestrels, ducks, squirrels, turtles and geckos.

Spy on the Vatican in the Orange Garden

On Aventine Hill, the southernmost of Rome's seven hills, oranges have pride of place in the Orange Garden (Giardino degli aranci), which is part of a park with a mesmerizing view across the entire city.

There's a special secret view you can discover in the park. Look for a simple iron gate with a keyhole, just outside the Priory of the Knights of Malta. Peep through the keyhole and you'll see a secret view of Saint Peter's Basilica dome peaking through the hedges.

If you can see Vatican City from the hilltop, you are looking across two countries at once! The park is also a venue for outdoor theatre performances.

The Orange garden is open from 8:30am to 6:30pm.

Find the Oldest Orange Tree

Among the Orange Garden's thousands of trees is a single descendant of the first orange tree planted on the hill. According to local legend, St. Dominic planted the first orange tree here more than 800 years ago. The original tree has long since perished, but a sapling from it must have taken root in its place. Can you find this special tree?

Hint: Look in the church yard of Santa Sabina.

A-Maze-ing Villa Doria Pamphili Gardens

Rome is a busy place with horns blaring as cars cram the narrow streets but you can escape the hustle and bustle in the tranquil gardens of the largest green space in the city, Villa Doria Pamphili.

Villa Doria is a seventeenth-century villa surrounded by a sprawling park and gardens with meandering paths taking you past monuments and along a lovely stream under the shade of many varieties of trees.

The villa's courtyard also has mazes made of hedges to find your way around.

Locals call this vast, manicured green space by its popular nickname, "Bel Respiro", meaning 'Deep Breath', because walking through the villa gardens is like taking a stroll through the countryside, where the air is always clean and refreshing, even though you are in the heart of a very busy city.

Picnic Spot Challenge

After exploring the vast park, you'll have surely worked up an appetite! So hunt down the perfect picnic spot for you and your family and friends to sit down for a feast.

Should it be by the fountain or overlooking the maze, or perhaps under the shade of a tree?

Exotic Encounters at Bioparco Zoo

Many exotic animals from around the world feel right at home in Rome's Bioparco Zoo, enjoying the sunny Italian summers, roaming about freely in enclosures that are like their natural habitats.

Plan to spend about four hours visiting all the different animal enclosures for mammals, reptiles, primates and birds living at the zoo. You can see lions and rhinos, plus a white tiger and a bear that now enjoy leisurely lives after being rescued from cruel conditions in captivity.

Seal ions, snakes, penguins and flamingos are part of the scenery, too, which includes a jungle with waterfalls for the troops of monkeys.

The zoo is open daily from 9:30am to 5:00pm.

Animal Tracker

The Bioparco Zoo is home to countless creatures of all shapes and sizes.

Keep a journal or notepad on hand and make notes of all the animals you see and write about the coolest creatures you find.

PART IV

Fortresses and Bravery Challenges

Learn about the legacy of Hadrian, one of Rome's most powerful emperors, and see if you're brave enough to visit the Catacombs and risk losing your hand in a deadly game of truth or dare!

Hadrian's Mausoleum

Hadrian's Mausoleum has many names. It's a fortress, a prison, military headquarters and museum, defending Rome on the bank of the River Tiber. The fortress also goes by the name 'Castel Sant'Angelo', or 'Castle of the Holy Angel'.

The mausoleum was built as the burial place of Hadrian, an Emperor who ruled the Roman Empire from 117 to 138. Hardrin is a big deal in Roman history, because his military and political prowess secured the Roman Empire within its existing borders, which then extended all the way to Hadrian's Wall in England, about 2,000 years ago.

Take a trip inside Hadrin's Mausoleum to learn what life in Rome was like 2,000 years ago in an immersive experience. The Passage of Boniface IX was once a prison. It now houses reconstructed medieval weapons and has a secret trap door. In the courtyard you can see more medieval war weapons used to defend the fortress in the past, including wooden catapults ready to lob metal balls over the walls.

The mausoleum is open Tuesday to Sunday from 9:00am to 7:30pm (last admission: 6:30pm).

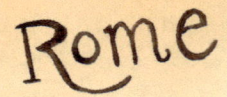

Rome

Fortress Exploring Adventure

There's nothing like climbing about an old castle to make you feel like an explorer in an adventure movie, so why not turn your trip to Castel Sant'Angelo into exactly that? Fire the cannons at the Bastions, visit the Armory and climb the tower to the top terrace to reach the best view in all of Italy!

Treasure Hunting in the Catacombs of Rome

Do you enjoy spooky tunnels filled with ancient secrets, and have you ever wondered where our ancient ancestors buried their dead?

Find out with an underground tour of the Roman Catacombs, a vast labyrinth of tunnels filled with religious art and buried treasures plus plenty of bones!

There are actually 60 separate catacombs in Rome, but only a handful of them are open to the public. These are the resting places of many Christian and Jewish saints and martyrs. The most popular catacombs open to the public are Catacombe di San Callisto, where you'll see religious art, including one of the earliest depictions of Jesus Christ, along with the tombs of bones.

Catacombe di San Callisto is open every day except Wednesday from 9:30am to 12:00pm, then again from 2:00pm to 5:00pm.

Earn a Bravery Badge

Being surrounded by bones in the narrow underground alleyways of the catacombs takes some guts. It's not for those of you that are easily spooked.

"Are the catacombs haunted?" you ask. Well, there's only one way to find out, isn't there?

If you survive the catacombs, you'll have earned yourself a bravery award, so why not make a bravery badge to show that you passed the scare test?

Dare You Test the Mouth of Truth?

In modern times, we have developed plenty of ways of determining the truth, from polygraphs and lie detectors to good old detective work. But the Romans had a very different and much more painful way of finding out whether someone was fibbing!

The Mouth of Truth (*Bocca della Verita*) is a large marble mask resembling a human face with an open mouth that's big enough to put your hand in.

No one knows for sure what it was for, but according to a local folklore, anyone suspected of lying could place a hand inside the mouth of the mask to prove it. if they were concealing a lie, their hand would be bitten off!

One version of the mask's history which may have some truth in it, is that the mask hid an executioner when suspected criminals were put on trial. If found guilty, the executioner behind the mask would chop off the criminal's hand.

You can try the Mouth of Truth yourself at Piazza Bocca della Verità, a short walk south from the Roman Forum, but think twice before you put your hand inside, in case you've told any fibs lately!

PART V

Pizza, Pasta & The World's First Ice Cream

Let's explore the pizzarias, pasta parlors and the sweet treats originating from Italy, including the first ice cream (gelato) ever made by an Italian architect, no less.

Gelato Fit for a Duke

The first ever ice cream was served in Italy more than 450 years ago during an opulent banquet hosted by the Duke of Florence. The duke tasked Italian architect Bernardo Buontalenti with creating a new dessert to impress his noble guests.

Bernardo whipped up the creamy concoction by blending frozen cream with lemon, sugar, egg, honey, milk, and a drop of wine.

Bernardo added flavors of bergamot and orange, calling it 'gelato'.

Today there are dozens of gelato flavors to choose from but the traditional flavor invented by Bernardo is the Buontalenti flavor, named after its creator, also known as 'crema fiorentina'.

Taste Test Adventure

How many gelaterias can you visit and how many different flavors can you try?

Make it a mission to see if you can rank the top ten gelato flavors.

A Slice of History Pizza

You probably already know that pizza is possibly the most popular classic Italian dish in the world but did you know that this fast food has a 2,000-year history dating back to ancient Rome?

Archeologists in Pompeii have found evidence of flatbreads covered in cheesy and fruity toppings as well as antique paintings depicting pizzas. Toppings have evolved over the centuries but it seems that Italians might have always had pineapple on their pizzas after all!

Here are three pizzerias in Rome where you can grab a slice or two of Italy's greatest export made the traditional way, of course:

Emma Pizzeria - the perfect place for a quick break from all your sightseeing

CasaMance - try a variety of toppings on small slices

Pinsa e Buoi - a classic Roman pizza experience

Rate Your Favorite Pizza Toppings

Eating pizza in Rome is the chance to try toppings you've never tasted before.

See how many different combos you can try, and make a list to rank the top-ten toppings of your trip.

Prehistoric Pasta Dinners in 300 BC

Italians have been having pasta for dinner since the 4th century BC so you can't possibly visit Rome without trying at least one or two authentic Italian pasta dishes. Varieties of pasta have evolved over the ages into dozens of shapes, from good old stringy spaghetti to fusilli twirls, penne tubes, bendy macaroni, ravioli pillows and many more in between.

The Italians have also invented dozens of pasta sauces, many of them taking advantage of Italy's endless supply of tomatoes. Here are three great pasta places to try in Rome:

- SantoPalato – serving classic Italian pasta dishes with a trendy twist
- Trecca-Roma – an authentic roman experience
- Trattoria al Moro – an old-school setting for modern taste buds

Rate Rome's Most Perfect Pasta

Whenever you dine on pasta in Rome, be sure you try a new dish each time, so you can explore new and exciting flavors – and maybe find a new favorite.

Take a pen and notebook with you so you can write down the restaurant you visit and some notes about the pasta dish that you tried.

Rate the restaurants and their pasta by giving each one a score out of 10.

Local Life at the Morning Market

Shop for fresh supplies with the locals at Campo de' Fiori Market on the east side of the River Tiber, about 1.5km from the Colosseum. Visiting this morning market is much like shopping in ancient Roman times with market stalls under tents selling fruit, vegetables, cheeses, meats and traditional street food snacks. It's a fine spot to enjoy the vibrant local life, sitting down with a snack in hand enjoying the view, live music and people watching.

Once you've filled up, you can take a short walk to visit nearby museums, including the famous Leonardo Da Vinci Museum. The market is open Monday to Saturday from 7:00am to 2:00pm.

Foodie Treasure Hunt

While scoping out the market, why not try a Foodie Treasure Hunt?

Make a list of 30 fruits and vegetables and tick off all the ones you can find at the Campo de Fiori market. Each tick is equal to one point. See how many points you can get!

Pastries and Cannoli: Sweet Surprises

Apart from ice cream, how many sweet treats and desserts from Italy have you heard of, and have you ever tried a fruit-topped panna cotta or a puffy pastry Zeppolle?

Crunchy Biscotti cookies and tiramisu are must-tries in Italy, too, but the most iconic Italian pastry to devour is Cannoli. It's a fried pastry shell filled to the brim with sweet ricotta cheese. Yum! Find plenty of sweet Italian treats at these three pastry shops in Rome:

- Regoli – one of the oldest pastry shops in Italy
- Biscottificio Innocenti – serving a wide variety of classic Italian cookies and biscuits
- Bompiani – traditional Italian pastries with a modern twist

Dessert Critic

Turn this sweet treat adventure into a game by trying as many different classic Italian desserts as you can.

Before your belly bursts, unleash your inner food critic and write a rant about each one you tried.

PART VI

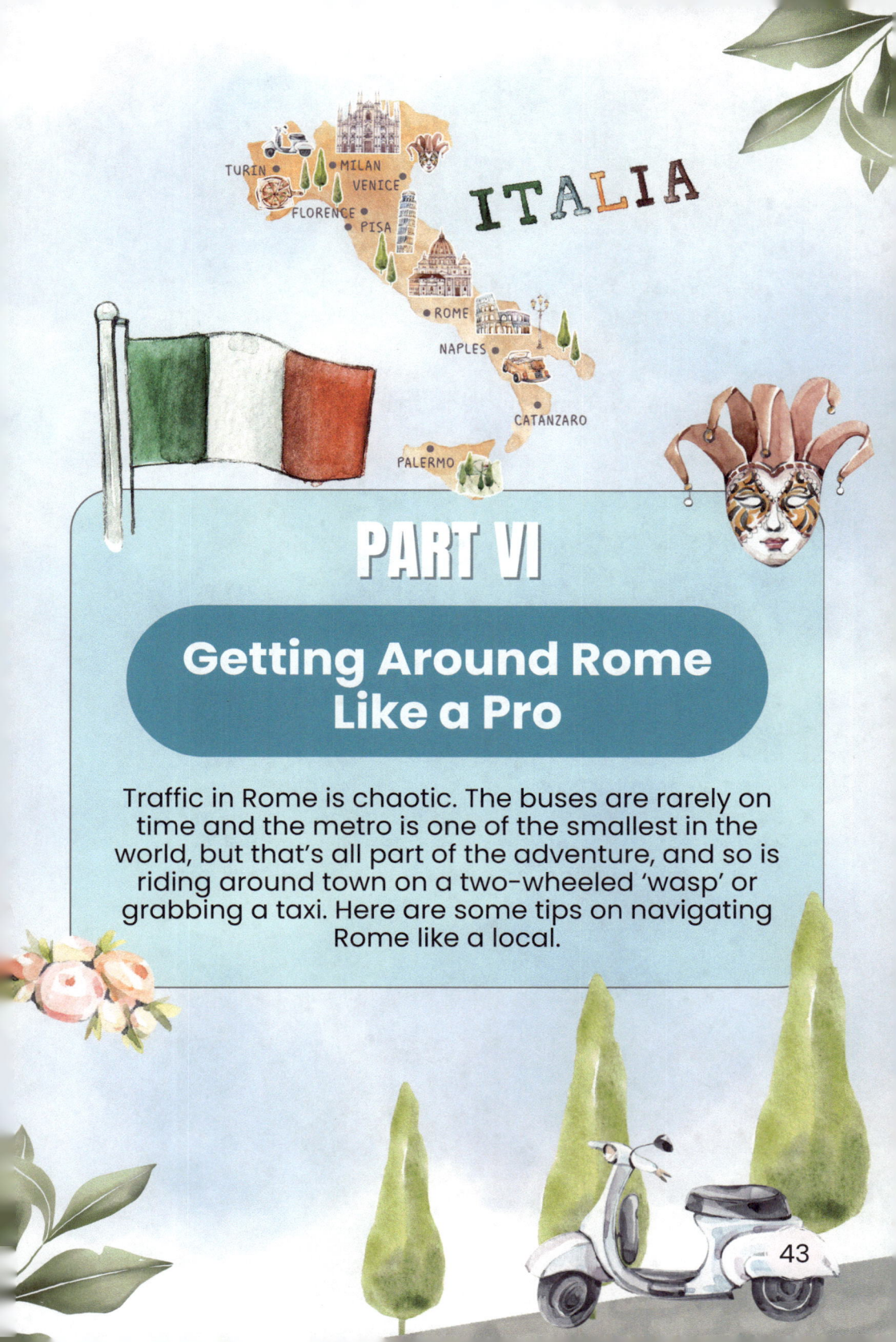

Getting Around Rome Like a Pro

Traffic in Rome is chaotic. The buses are rarely on time and the metro is one of the smallest in the world, but that's all part of the adventure, and so is riding around town on a two-wheeled 'wasp' or grabbing a taxi. Here are some tips on navigating Rome like a local.

Boarding Buses and the Metro

Like any huge city, Rome has robust public transport systems in place designed to help you get around quickly and easily. This includes over 338 bus lines and a Metro, which means you will always have plenty of options to travel from one exciting place to another.

Rome Bus Routes

Rome has 8,260 bus stops. Luckily for young globetrotters and adventurers like you, many of these stops are located near some of Rome's most popular sites and attractions.

Don't expect the buses in Rome to arrive at stops on schedule. They often run a bit late as they navigate the city's chaotic streets. But even though punctuality isn't their strong suit, the buses are a reliable way of getting around safely with locals and visitors alike making frequent use of them.

Just be sure to hold your parents' hands at all times.

If you plan to use the buses to get around Rome, buying an all-purpose travel card makes traveling convenient by allowing you on any bus at any time during your stay. You should also get to know the different types of bus lines marked by letters. They include:

- **Urban lines (U)**

    These are the most common, and run from 5:00am to 12:00pm.

- **Night buses (N)**

    These operate during the hours when urban lines are inactive, late at night.

- **Express (X)**

    These lines are designed for longer journeys, usually to the outskirts of Rome.

- **Exact (E)**

    These lines link Rome's centre to the surrounding neighborhoods, and are the most reliable due to running on fixed timetables.

Wait at a designated bus stop to catch a bus. Don't worry if you don't immediately see your bus when you arrive. It's not uncommon for buses in Rome to be more than 30 minutes late.

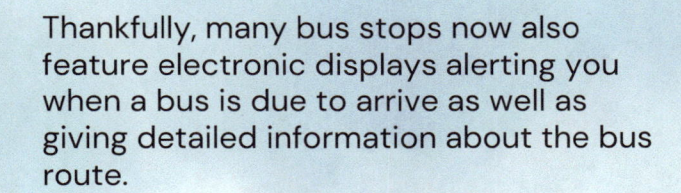

Thankfully, many bus stops now also feature electronic displays alerting you when a bus is due to arrive as well as giving detailed information about the bus route.

Another neat bus stop feature to make sure you catch the right bus is announcements when a bus is on the way or departing. The announcements are only spoken in Italian so here are a some key phrases to help you:

- **"In arrivo"** – the bus is arriving soon.

- **"3 Fer 2"** – the bus is 3 stops away and will arrive in 2 minutes.

- **"A capolinea"** – the bus has arrived at the first stop along its route.

When you climb aboard a bus, just remember to validate your ticket.

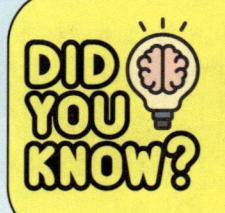

DID YOU KNOW? Rome is known as the 'Eternal City' because people believe it will never fall or be destroyed.

Rome Metro

Rome's Metro system is actually one of the smallest in Europe so it's not always as reliable as the buses, and may not reach your destination. Still, it's important to know how to use the Metro if you ever need to hop on a train in a pinch.

Spotting the metro stations is easy. Just look for a Metro station sign with a big white M on a red background.

Once inside a metro station, buy tickets from ticket kiosks or machines that resemble ATMs. Not all stations have ticket machines.

With your ticket in hand, you can now board the train, after passing through the turnstile.

Keep hold of your ticket because sometimes inspectors wait to check tickets at Metro exits.

But wait! How do you know which train to board?

Ciao

The Rome Metro has three lines – Line A (orange), Line B (blue) and Line C (green) – displayed on metro maps.

Each line stops at different stations but all the lines intersect at the central Termini station, where you can change lines to reach your destination.

Before you board the train, make sure your destination shows as 'Live' on the train's list of stops. This means that the train is still headed in that direction.

If it shows as 'Not Live', that means the train has already passed that stop.

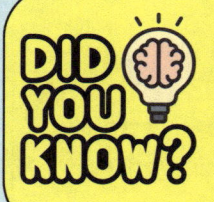

DID YOU KNOW? About 820,000 passengers use the Rome Metro each day. Over an entire year, that amounts to about 320 million passengers.

Vespas: The Wasps of Rome

Vespa mopeds are a popular way to zip around the winding streets of Rome. After all, the Vespa is an iconic Italian motorbike and is as much a part of the culture as pasta and pizzas.

If you have a valid international driving license, you can rent a Vespa to explore Rome on two wheels like a local. Vespa is the Italian word for 'wasp', which is quite fitting given the small size and buzzing sound that these motorbikes make.

The first Vespa was designed in the early 20th century by aviation engineer and designer Corradino D'Ascanio, who had designed his own glider by age 15 and became responsible for the manufacture of Italy's first helicopter. The company Piaggio, which made boats and aircraft, commissioned D'Ascanio to design an all-Italian motorbike.

Mr D'Ascanio didn' like the look of regular motorcycles. He thought they were rugged and ugly, so he came up with the sleek Vespa design for Piaggio, and it became the most copied design in the world.

Taxi Hailing Tips

Getting around Rome in a taxi can be quicker and more reliable than waiting for a bus or riding the Metro. Taxis are much more comfortable too!

You shouldn't try hailing taxis from the roadside. Head to an official taxi stand instead.

All Rome taxis are colored white with a bright orange 'Taxi' sign lit up when available. If there aren't any taxis at the stand, just wait for one to pull up. Alternatively you can download a taxi-hailing app. Trusted taxi apps you can use in Rome include: appTaxi, Uber, FreeNow, and ItTaxi.

Types of Taxis

There are generally three types of taxi operating in Rome.

Standard taxis comfortably seat four passengers. You should see the driver's name displayed on the car, plus the license number and the municipality's symbol on the front doors and on the left rear door.

Van taxis can normally fit up to seven passengers, which is ideal for big families and luggage, plus you enjoy more leg room without having to sit on top of each other.

There are several wheelchair accessible taxi services in Rome, which can be found online. They may be classified as a limo service, so the vans may be a color other than white.

Taxi Etiquette

Etiquette is important if you plan on making use of one of Rome's many great taxi services. These are the guidelines you should follow to ensure that you do not offend anyone on your trip. Luckily, they are very simple.

- **Respect queues.** Many people use taxi services in Rome, so it's polite to wait your turn before getting into a cab. Don't jump the queue!

- **Be polite:** Always greet your driver and make sure that you clearly specify your destination. Thank them as you leave.

- **Tip if you like:** You don't have to tip taxi drivers but if you enjoyed a friendly service, then it's fine to thank the driver by paying a little extra on top of the fare as a tip.

Bridges and Boat Rides on the Tiber River

At more than 252 miles long, the Tiber River is the second longest river in Italy, twisting and turning through the centre of Rome, dividing the city into east and west sides of the river as it makes its way to the south coast of Italy.

There are a total of 28 bridges crossing the Tiber to connect the two sides of the capital.

The oldest and best-preserved Roman bridge is the stone Fabrician Bridge (Ponte Fabricio), connecting Tiberine Island to the left bank of the Tiber since 62 BC.

Boat rides are a leisurely way to explore the city. You can book boat tours near tourist attractions such as Tiber Island, Sant'Angelo Bridge, Palazzo di Giustizia, Piazza del Popolo, and Vatican City.

You can also take a hop-on, hop-off riverboat, allowing you to explore landmarks at your leisure.

PART VII

Getting Acquainted with Real Roman Culture

Traveling to a different country is always exciting with sights and sounds we've never experienced before, so let's really get to know the creative side of modern day Rome and learn a bit of the local lingo.

Italian Theatre: From Opera to Street Performers

Rome has been the hub of Italy's rich heritage of artistic expression since the renaissance period, which gave rise to some of the world's most talented painters, musicians, architects and mathematicians. This Roman tradition of innovation extends to its theatre scene as well.

Rome's theatrical origins are rooted in ancient Greece with many of the country's traditions propagated by the Romans. In many ways, the Colosseum – with its boisterous displays of martial combat – was a form of brutal theatre, but it wasn't until much later during the Renaissance that Roman and Italian theatre would finally come into its own.

Street performers were already popular before 1500. They would perform on makeshift stages with very little in the way of set design, capitalizing on acrobatic abilities, singing voices and the ability to tell a riveting story with epic poetry committed to memory or through reenactments of classical Greek comedies.

These performances became more sophisticated over the years and by 1650, Italian theatre had evolved to resemble the kind of performances we enjoy today.

The Artists and Fountains of Piazza Navona

Rome has many famous streets and squares, but none are quite as iconic and unique as Piazza Navona. If you want to fully immerse yourself in the artistic culture of Rome, Piazza Navona is the place to do it.

Piazza Navona was originally developed as a stadium of sorts, way back in the first century AD, hosting athletic competitions and games. However, as these sports faded in popularity, the square's purpose shifted to become a bustling market.

The square's most recognisable features are its three gorgeous fountains: Fountain of the Four Rivers; Seashell Fountain; and the Fountain of Neptune.

The 17th-century Baroque church of Sant'Agnese in Agone flanks the square, and is worth a visit to see the skull of St. Agnes and learn the story of her martyrdom.

On summer nights, the square becomes a vibrant venue filled with street performers and vendors peddling their wares.

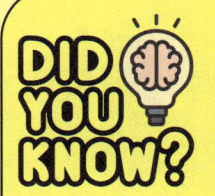

DID YOU KNOW? Rome is home to the world's oldest shopping mall, Trajan's Market, which was built nearly 2,000 years ago and had over 150 shops.

Across the Tiber to Timeless Trastevere

By now you should have an agenda full of exciting museums and attractions to visit while in Rome, but you haven't truly experienced the essence of Roman life until you've had a taste of Trastevere – an ideal destination for a family meal that won't cost an arm and a leg.

Trastevere is a charming part of the city and the perfect place to truly appreciate the local way of life away from the crowded tourist destinations on the map.

The name Trastevere comes from two words that mean 'across the Tiber', because it's away from the city center, on the west side of the Tiber River.

This historic neighbourhood was originally inhabited by sailors and fishermen and is today full of bars and restaurants offering local delights at local prices.

Walking the cobbled streets and watching the locals go about their daily lives is an authentic insight into rustic Rome that Julius Caesar once called home.

Italian Slang for Kids: Talk like a real Roman

If you're going to spend time in Italy, you should certainly learn how to speak some of the local lingo. Italian slang has a unique aural quality to it, making it always sounds sophisticated no matter what context you use it in.

Here are some of the most popular Italian slang phrases you should know:

- **"Paisan"** – to refer to a fellow Italian or someone of Italian descent.

- **"Mamma mia"** – known all over the world to express shock or surprise.

- **"Prego"** – a courteous way to say thanks or welcome, depending on the context.

- **"Bambino"** – an affectionate term for a young child, such as your younger sibling.

- **"Capisce"** – directly translates as 'understand?'

Of course this is just a handful of the many Italian phrases you can learn and practice when in Rome.

You can find more useful phrases in the appendix of this book, which you can practice before arriving or while you're traveling.

Rome's Modern Murals & Street Art

Many of the modern areas of Rome are home to a fantastic assortment of street art, proving that the city's artistic traditions haven't slowed down since the heyday of the Italian Renaissance. Below is a list of the best neighbourhoods to explore if you're in search of some stunning modern day murals:

- Tor Marancia
- Porto Fluviale
- Opera Muri Sicuri di Carlos Atoche
- Via delle Conce
- Museo dell'Altro e dell'Altrove di Metropoliz Città Meticcia

Of course, there is plenty of street art to be found all throughout your adventures in Rome, so make sure you keep a camera handy to take some photos of them all!

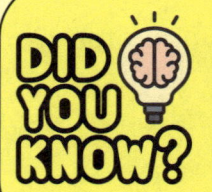

DID YOU KNOW?

When wandering around the city you often find yourself walking on the stones of ancient Roman roads laid more than 2,000 years ago.

PART VIII

Day Trips and Excursions from Rome

Have a blast exploring volcanic Pompeii and Emperor Hadrian's Palace plus other timeless attractions beyond the walled city of Rome for an adventurous family day out.

Frozen in Time Under the Ashes of Pompeii

The tragic tale of Pompeii, about 250 km south of Rome, is a story of apocalyptic proportions. The city sits at the foot of the volcano Mount Vesuvius, which trapped its inhabitants in a shower of volcanic ash and debris when it erupted more than 2,000 years ago.

The eruption occurred on the 24th of August, 79 CE, rapidly covering the entire city in a deep layer of ash and filling the air with poisonous gases, killing the city's entire population and freezing them in time.

The ash and pumice that rained down from the massive eruption buried the city in a layer up to six meters deep, miraculously preserving much of its infrastructure and architecture, as well as the shapes of the people trapped in their homes, until the city was unearthed centuries later when explorers uncovered its remains in the 1700s.

The explorers were astounded to find the ancient roman town's houses and temples still perfectly intact. In fact they even found loaves of bread in the ovens. The entire city was frozen in time, now giving us a first-hand glimpse of Italian life millennia ago.

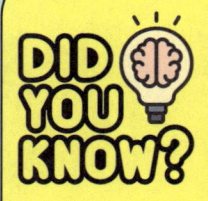

DID YOU KNOW? The people trapped in the volcanic ash that fell on Pompeii were not preserved, but their bodies left voids in the ash as they decayed. Archeologists then made plaster casts of the voids.

Emperor Hadrian's Villa and Palaces

Villas were a status symbol of wealth and power in Ancient Rome, but many have decayed or been damaged over the centuries. But none are better preserved than Hadrian's Villa, a vast, lavish estate covering over 250 acres about 30 km east of Rome that once belonged to Emperor Hadrian.

The villa estate is made up of 30 separate buildings surrounded by beautiful gardens, decorative fountains, swimming pools with cascading waterfalls, libraries, and military barracks.

Hadrian ruled over Rome during the 2nd century AD, choosing this location for his country home because of the abundant water supply. Simply put, he never had to go far for a quick dip in the pool.

The villa has been remarkably well preserved, and you can easily book a day trip to see it up close for yourself. The gardens are enchanting and you can even see inside Hadrian's personal island retreat, which included his own private chambers and chamber pot.

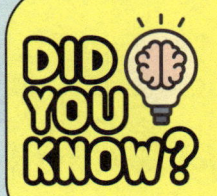

DID YOU KNOW? Hadrian is considered one of Rome's 'Five Good Emperors', because he cared for the people, spent the empire's money wisely, and strengthened the empire.

Exploring Enchanting Castles

Just outside Rome you can explore many well-preserved castles and ancient Roman camps (castrum) which were established when the Roman Empire was flourishing over a thousand years ago.

Similar to Pompeii, the area at the foot of the volcanic Alban Hills, about 20 km southeast of Rome, is stunningly picturesque with villas and fortresses nestled among sprawling vineyards that have preserved their quintessentially Italian rustic charm. The region is great for growing grapes because the volcanic ash in the soil makes it rich in minerals – a natural fertilizer.

Ostia Antica – The Oldest Seaport

Your trip to Rome will probably be by plane, train or automobile, but back in the days of yore, those wishing to visit the Italian capital would arrive by boat. In those days there may have been a few tourists but most of those arriving would be traders from around the world, bringing herbs, spices, cloth and precious cargoes to Ancient Rome's bustling seaport, Ostia Antica.

Today Ostia Antica is a much quieter place than before. Its origins can be traced back as far as the 4th century BC, making it one of Rome's oldest preserved sites.

The old port features many of the architectural stylings of Pompeii but it's a much quieter place to visit, making it perfect for enjoying classical Roman architecture without all the hustle and bustle of more popular tourist attractions.

PART IX

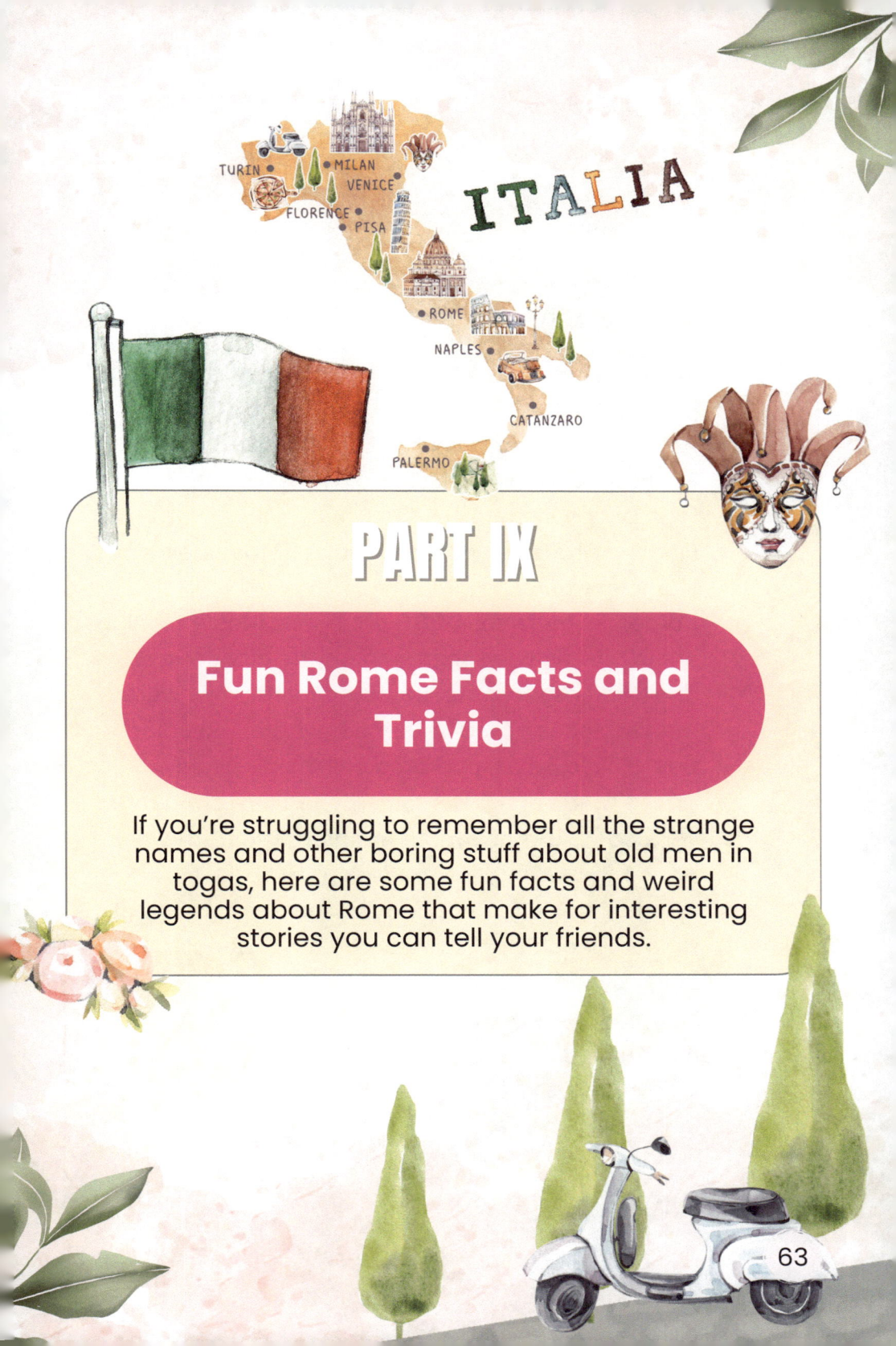

Fun Rome Facts and Trivia

If you're struggling to remember all the strange names and other boring stuff about old men in togas, here are some fun facts and weird legends about Rome that make for interesting stories you can tell your friends.

Mind-Boggling Rome Trivia to Impress Your Friends

Here are some fun facts about Rome that not many people know. Use these to impress your friends!

- Rome has more than 2,000 fountains – more than anywhere else in the world.
- Around 3,000 euros are collected from Trevi Fountain every night from coins tossed into the fountain by visitors.
- Flamingo tongues were a popular Roman delicacy in ancient times.
- Rome has more than 900 churches, most of which are located close together near the city centre.
- The Romans invented shopping malls. They were marketplaces called 'tabernae', where you could buy wine, clothes, and bread all in one place.
- All the roads in the Roman empire were connected via a complex network directing traffic to the city. Hence the saying, "All roads lead to Rome".
- Women in ancient Rome dyed their hair with goat fat and beech wood ashes. The most popular colours were red and blonde.
- La Sapienza was the first university in Rome. It's also the largest university in Rome and the second largest in the world.
- Rome once had a National Museum of Pasta.

Famous Roman Rulers and Artists

Rome has been home to many of the world's most brilliant minds. You'll have heard of some of them such as Rome's most famous statesman and emperor Julius Caesar, because he was a dictator who was partially responsible for the fall of Rome, yet more than 77 emperors ruled the empire between 27 BC and 476 AD.

A handful of Roman emperors were considered 'The Five Good Emperors of Rome'. They were Nerva, Trajan, Antoninus Pius, Hadrian, and Marcus Aurelius. They were revered for being stoic and fair leaders, making Rome a prosperous capital while fostering intellectualism, philosophy and creativity.

As creativity flourished during the Italian Renaissance, artists such as Raphael, Leonardo da Vinci, and Michelangelo came to the fore, leaving us with the world's most celebrated masterpieces in the form of otherworldly architecture and paintings.

One of the best ways to find out about all the other important people in Ancient Roman history is to visit the museums in which their statues and art pieces now stand.

See what you can find out about these other famous Romans:

- Mark Antony
- Agrippa
- Cleopatra
- Hadrian
- Nero
- Titus

Strange Roman Laws and Traditions

The ancient world was full of strange laws, customs, and traditions – many of them originating in Ancient Rome as the empire sought to rule the world.

Here are some of the weirdest laws and traditions that ancient Romans once lived by:

- Wearing purple was a crime because lower-class people were not allowed to display any signs of wealth; purple being one of them.
- Women were not allowed to cry at funerals.
- People that died from a lightning strike were not allowed to be buried.
- The ultimate punishment was to be put in a sack with wild animals.
- It was not impolite to burp when eating. In fact it was encouraged to show your appreciation for the fine food.

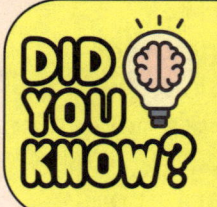

DID YOU KNOW? The Romans had heated swimming pools at public bathhouses, which were open to all for relaxing with friends and doing business.

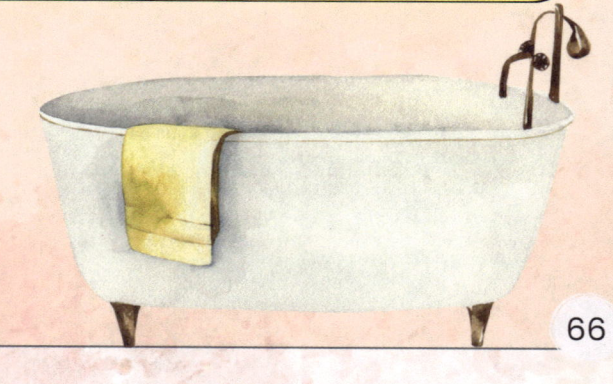

The Legend of Wolf Children Romulus and Remus

According to legend, Rome was founded by two brothers, Romulus and Remus. They were apparently abandoned in the wild as babies and left to the elements but were soon found by a female wolf, who nursed the two brothers to health until they were found by a shepherd called Fasutulusand and his wife, Acca Larentia.

The brothers were both natural born leaders. As they grew older they became wise and ambitious with a shared desire to establish a city. Unfortunately they quarrelled over where the city should be built, leading to a fight in which Romulus killed his brother. Romulus went on to establish Rome on Palatine Hill, naming the city after himself.

This story perfectly encapsulates the Roman spirit with its themes of destiny and greatness. But how much of it is true? Nobody really knows but it's a cool story that has captured artists' imaginations for millennia.

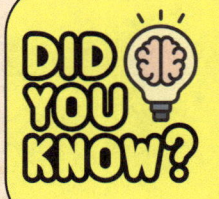

> **DID YOU KNOW?** A statue of Romulus and Remus as babies drinking milk from a she-wolf is one of the oldest in the world. It stands in the Palazzo dei Conservatori on Capitoline Hill.

PART X

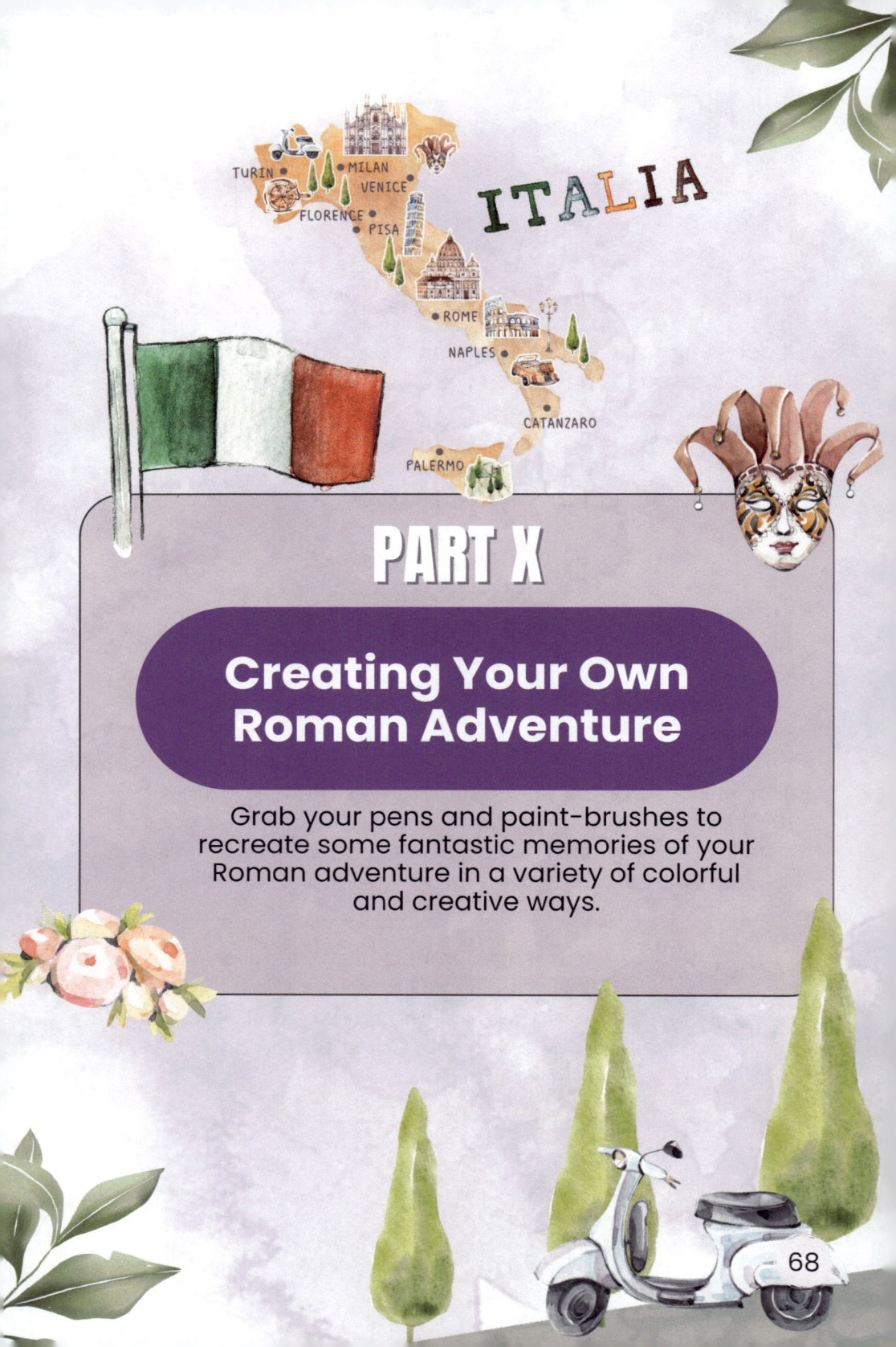

Creating Your Own Roman Adventure

Grab your pens and paint-brushes to recreate some fantastic memories of your Roman adventure in a variety of colorful and creative ways.

Make Your Own Rome Scrapbook

For this activity you'll need an empty workbook, some glue, pens, and highlighters, plus some photos taken during your trip or pictures cut out from old newspapers or magazines.

Start by decorating the cover of your scrap book with wrapping paper and decorate it some more with one of the pictures you've chosen.

Write a title on the cover such as 'My Rome Scrapbook'.

Fill the inside of the book with pages dedicated to different parts of your adventure.

For example, you could dedicate a two-page spread to your visit to the Sistine Chapel, and another spread to Pompeii.

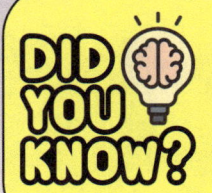

DID YOU KNOW? You'll see wild cats all over Rome, roaming free and snoozing among the ruins, because they are protected by a law established in 1991.

Roman Memory Lane Journal Prompts

Your adventure in Rome will probably have left you with some wonderful memories so why not keep them in a journal? Use the journaling prompts on the following pages to write about your memories of Rome while they're still fresh in your mind.

1. Which museum was your favorite and why?

2. Out of all the artwork you saw, which was your favorite?

3. Describe the sights and sounds you remember most vividly about your trip to Rome.

_____
_____
_____
_____
_____
_____
_____

4. What food did you like the most in Rome?

_____
_____
_____
_____
_____
_____
_____

5. How did you get about in Rome?
   Tell us about one of your trips on a bus, the metro or in a taxi.

6. What would you ask a famous Italian artist if you could go back in time?
   Write your questions and the answers you imagine you might get.

Design Your Own Roman Crest or Shield

Crests were a symbol of wealth and status in Ancient Roman times, just as they still are among nobility today. Similarly, shields denoted a person's military rank, which came with a ton of respect itself. Crests and shields often shared similar imagery such as eagles and wreaths of olive leaves, all depicted in a unique, ornate style.

With this in mind, imagine how your own crest or shield would look. You don't have to use eagles and wreaths. You could use hyenas and forks if you like! The imagery you choose is up to you, but try to design your crest or shield in the traditional Roman style.

Design Here

Draw Your Favorite Roman Landmark

With so many famous landmarks to explore in Rome, you should have plenty of memories and hundreds of photos to flip through.

Which one stands out as your favorite and can you draw it from memory or by copying one of the photos you took?

Draw Here

Write a Postcard to Your Future Self

Wherever you go on holiday anywhere, you should send someone a postcard, so be sure to grab a few to send to friends back home. On this page though, practice by writing a postcard to your future self so you can look back in years to come of your incredible adventure.

POST CARD

Plan Your Next Roman Adventure

With so much to see and do in Rome, you probably haven't had time to fit it all into one trip. We hope you managed to at least try some pizza and gelato! But if there is anything you didn't do or try during your trip, write a list below of plans for your next visit. Think hard and try to include as many details as you can, such as how you'll get there.

_____
_____
_____
_____
_____

MORE ROME MEMORY LANE JOURNAL PROMPTS

1. When you first arrived in Rome, what did you see, hear, and smell?

   _____
   _____
   _____
   _____
   _____
   _____
   _____

2. Tell us a story about something hilarious that happened to you during your Roman adventure.

   _____
   _____
   _____
   _____
   _____
   _____

3. Write about your visit to a famous Ancient Roman landmark such as the Colosseum or the Roman Forum. What was your favorite part?

_____
_____
_____
_____
_____
_____
_____
_____

4. Describe something interesting you learned about Rome's rich history.

_____
_____
_____
_____
_____
_____

5. If you visited a museum in Rome, write about an exhibit that fascinated you and why.

6. If you visited a park in Rome, describe what you did and saw there.

7. Write about the most interesting food you tried in Rome, describing how it tasted.

8. How did you get around the city?
Write about your experience riding the metro or taking a bus or taxi.

9. Who was the most interesting person you met in Rome? Write about your interaction with them.

10. Describe a busy street or market you visited. What sights, sounds, and smells can you remember?

11. What has been your favorite moment in Rome so far?
    Write about why it was so special.

Appendix

You're nearly at the end of the book but read on to learn some useful phrases in Italian plus some book and movie recommendations about Rome that'll be fun to read and watch now that you're familiar with the ancient city.

Useful Italian Phrases for Young Travelers

- **Please** – *Per favore* (pronounced 'Per-fah-vo-reh')

- **Thank you** – *Grazie*

- **You're welcome** – *Prego*

- **Good morning or Good day** – *Buongiorno* (pronounced 'bon-jor-no')

- **Good night or Good evening** – *Buonasera* (pronounced 'bwana-sera')

- **Goodbye** – Arrivederci (pronounced 'aribe-dechi')

- **I like** – Mi piace (pronounced 'me-pia-chu')

- **Where is** – Dov'e...? (pronounced 'dov-eh')

- **How much?** – Quanto Costa?

Ciao

Books and Movies About Rome for Kids

Books:

♥ *What It Was Like to Be an Ancient Roman* by David Long and Stefano Tambellini

♥ *A Gladiator Stole My Lunchbox* by Thiago de Moraes

♥ *Escape From Pompeii* by Christina Balit

♥ *My Family and Other Romans* by Marie Basting

♥ *The Magnificent Book of Treasures: Ancient Rome* by Stella Caldwell and Eugenia Nobati

Movies:

♥ *Roman Holiday (1953)* dir. William Wyler

♥ *When in Rome (2002)* dir. Steve Purcell

♥ *The Thief Lord (2006)* dir. Richard Claus

♥ *Only You (1994)* dir. Norman Jewison

♥ *The Agony and the Ecstasy (1965)* dir. Carol Reed

Made in the USA
Columbia, SC
21 March 2025